PART VI.

1 K

EXPLORATIONS AND SURVEYS FOR A RAILROAD ROUTE FROM THE MISSISSIPPI RIVER TO THE PACIFIC OCEAN.

WAR DEPARTMENT.

ROUTE NEAR THE THIRTY-FIFTH PARALLEL, EXPLORED BY LIEUT. A. W. WHIPPLE, TOPOGRAPHICAL ENGINEERS, IN 1853 AND 1854.

REPORT

ON

THE ZOOLOGY OF THE EXPEDITION.

WASHINGTON, D. C.
1856.

No. 1.

FIELD NOTES AND EXPLANATIONS.

BY C. B. R. KENNERLY, M. D.,

PHYSICIAN AND NATURALIST TO THE EXPEDITION.

WASHINGTON, D. C., *July* 1, 1854.

SIR: I have the honor herewith to present a general account of the game animals of the country traversed by you in surveying a route for the railroad to the Pacific. I do not propose here to go into much detail, as the description of the individual species, with an account of their characteristic habits, is reserved for a subsequent report. For convenience of reference, I shall divide the line into several portions, and express, as briefly as possible, the peculiar features in the economical zoology of each.

From the Rio Grande to Zuñi.—Although this district is hunted very closely by Indians and other persons traversing it, yet in some places we found game abundant. Before reaching the pueblo of Laguna, however, animals of the larger kind were rarely observed, the country being for the most part quite open, and affording but little permanent water. Still, along the road, the large rabbit of this region (*Lepus callotis*) and the smaller species (*Lepus artemesiæ*) were found in considerable numbers; and, after reaching the Rio Rito, to these were added ducks and geese in great numbers. But after leaving this village, and approaching the Sierra Madre, we found ourselves in a country heavily wooded, and with an abundance of grass. Here we observed numerous herds of the black-tailed deer (*Cervus macrotis*) feeding in the little valleys; and, among the bushes on the hill-sides, several species of bears, the black (*Ursus Americanus*) and the huge grizzly, (*Ursus ferox.*) Among the trees in the mountain, the piñon (*Pinus edulis*) was very common, which affords a kind of nut on which the latter animals delight to feed, and it is not unpalatable even to man. This district has long been celebrated for its game, and the accounts that we heard proved not to be exaggerated.

Descending the western slope of the mountains, we again met with rabbits in great numbers. Besides these, we occasionally found the antelope; but being much hunted, they were here scarce and wild, and, when seen, were far off in small herds upon the plain. Along the valleys that stretch towards the pueblo of Zuñi, and which are generally hemmed in by rough and rugged hills, we found the grizzly bear (*Ursus ferox*) abundant. When impelled by hunger, they become very fierce, and, descending into the valleys, frighten off the *pastores*, who, in their terror, abandon their flocks to these huge monsters.

A part of this country abounds in birds of many varieties; among the lofty pines and thick cedars of the Sierra Madre, we were enabled to collect many valuable specimens of new and otherwise interesting species.

From the pueblo of Zuñi to the Little Colorado river.—Leaving the village, we continued our march for a short distance along the Zuñi creek, making, as we went, interesting collections of fishes, mostly new and undescribed species. Leaving the creek then to our left, we passed through a succession of cedar groves and grassy valleys, abounding in black-tailed deer and antelopes, (*Antilo capra Americana.*) In this region we first saw signs of the panther. This animal prefers the hill-sides or ravines, where the bushes are the thickest and most impenetrable, and rarely shows itself during the day on the open plain, unless forced there by hunger to hunt rabbits or other animals upon which it feeds. At night the prairie jackal, or coyote, (*Canis latrans*) rarely failed to approach our camp, and serenade us with his loud and varied notes. The long and dismal howl of the larger species (*Canis gigas*) was occasionally heard in the distance; but the latter is much less numerous than the former, and was not often seen. It, too, prefers the wooded regions, and depends mainly upon the deer for a subsistence, which it hunts, and rarely fails, after a long pursuit, in overtaking and conquering. In many places birds were scarce, yet we were enabled to collect some very interesting specimens. The weather being cold, the reptiles had all disappeared.

From Little Colorado to Pueblo creek.—Passing down the Little Colorado, we often saw ducks of the commoner kind—mallard and teal; but these were not so numerous as we expected. The cause may be found, perhaps, in the fact that along that portion of the valley over which we passed there were no marshes or flats, and the kinds of vegetable matter on which they feed were almost entirely wanting. Nor did the stream in that part furnish fish in great numbers; for, notwithstanding our frequent attempts to catch a few with our nets for specimens, we succeeded in taking only one. The beaver, (*Castor fiber,*) however, was very common in many places, as well as the Canada porcupine, (*Hystrix canadensis.*) They find a bountiful subsistence in the bark and tender twigs and buds of the young cottonwood trees, (*Populus,*) which grow luxuriantly in the sandy soil of the river bottom.

After leaving the Little Colorado, we turned directly towards the San Francisco mountain, its summit, at this season, (December,) covered with snow. Ascending the gravelly mesa, our train passed slowly on, occasionally turning from a direct line to avoid a small hill or little cañon. As we ascended, in approaching the mountain, we suffered not a little from the cold and piercing wind, from which there was no escape. The little valleys skirting its eastern base, supplying good grass, were now the resort of hundreds of antelopes, which were here also partly sheltered by the neighboring hills. This mountain is covered with a dense forest of pine, among which we found, in great numbers, the beautiful tufted squirrel, (*Sciurus aberti.*) This interesting animal we had not observed before; nor did we find it further west than this range. Wild turkeys were common, also, in the same locality. Ascending high into the mountains, we found many tracks of the big-horn, (*Ovis montana;*) but notwithstanding our repeated efforts to secure one, we were unsuccessful. The timidity of this animal causes it to dwell in the most inaccessible places.

A few short marches through dense pine forests and the deep snow brought us near Mount Sitgreaves, from the base of which stretched beautiful valleys, covered with grass, and dotted by clumps of cedars. This mountain had been, apparently, before the falling of the snow, the peculiar home of grizzly bears; but the cold and want of food had caused them all to go in search of other quarters. The number of trails of this animal that we found here, all leading towards the south, is almost incredible.

From this point our journey lay, for some days, along beautiful valleys, and often through thick and dark forests of cedars; and as we marched along we reaped a rich harvest of the smaller quadrupeds, such as pouched rats, mice, &c. Nor were we compelled to lay aside our rifles for want of larger game; for, although we saw no antelopes, the black-tailed deer was here quite common, and not very shy, being unaccustomed to the sight of man. Reaching soon a handsome valley, with its surface cut by a serpentine cañon—at some seasons, probably, containing a running stream, but now only watered by a succession of cool and clear pools—we found, in great numbers, Gambel's partridge, (*Callipepla Gambellii.*) While encamped here this beautiful bird afforded us fine sport with our shot-guns, and furnished us with many delicious meals. Along this cañon were many deserted wigwams, the Indians having probably retired to the south at the approach of winter.

This immediate region being hilly, and covered, for the most part, by bushes, was not a spot well suited to the habits of the antelope, and hence we did not find it here. This species prefers the open valley, or wide and unbroken plain. Descending into the Chino valley, we found this animal in large herds, sometimes of hundreds. Occasionally, impelled by curiosity, they would approach quite near, and for a time gaze upon the train, then circling round, would hurry off and disappear in the distance. Indeed, the apparent curiosity of this animal is one of its marked peculiarities, and the western hunter often takes advantage of it to lure the unsuspecting creature within reach of his rifle.

After leaving the Chino valley, we entered again the cedar forests, where we found wild turkeys once more very abundant, frequenting, for the most part, the neighborhood of the little brooks that we found in this region, and feeding upon the berries of the rough-barked and other species of cedar.

In the thick underbrush along these creeks we often found the beds and resting places of the grizzly bear; but the animal itself we never saw. In this vicinity we caught some interesting fishes, and collected many handsome specimens of birds, the smaller species, particularly, being quite numerous.

From Pueblo creek to Williams' river.—Following up Pueblo creek nearly to its source in the mountains, we passed through Aztec Pass. This was a beautiful little stream, and we were sorry to leave it, as in this region one seldom sees such cool and limpid water.

Passing through the mountain, we again descended into a beautiful valley, where we found both the black-tailed deer and antelope quite numerous. Continuing our march, we crossed, from time to time, deep cañons with their pools of clear water, though containing no fishes, yet affording a sporting place for many ducks. The sides of these cañons are composed of rugged and precipitous cliffs, in which the lynx (*Lynx rufus*) and other wild animals of this region live. The caves, also, among these rocks often afford shelter for the wild Indians of this region, who gather the maguey plant, (*Agave Americana,*) which grows in great luxuriance here, and store it away for winter use. This is their principal food, although they combine with it the flesh of mice, rats, and such other animals as they can capture.

The distance from Pueblo creek to Williams' river is probably much less than the distance embraced between any other divisions that we have assumed; but it was a country throughout particularly rich in deer. It was a country, also, pretty well wooded with the various species of cedar, which, in addition to its affording a shelter for the larger animals, supplied also, in their berries, food for various species of the smaller birds, some interesting specimens of which we were enabled to collect. We frequently passed the burrows of the smaller quadrupeds, with their heaps of spiny cactaceæ piled over them to prevent the coyote from destroying them and their habitations. The long and barbed spines of this plant are sufficient to deter the wolf from committing his depredations, but the small rabbit, (*Lepus artemesiæ,*) not resorting to this important expedient for protection, often falls a victim to the rapacity of this animal by being chased or scented to its burrow and then dug out. The jackass rabbit, (*Lepus callotis,*) being much more swift than the small one, is less liable to be overtaken by its untiring enemy.

From Williams' river to the Great Colorado river.—We entered here upon a district of new character and of much interest. Descending into the valley of this stream, and travelling along its banks to its confluence with Rio Santa Maria, we had an opportunity of seeing, as well as collecting, many new and interesting objects; among the larger game recognizing many old acquaintances whose forms had now become familiar. On the wide mesas that stretched out on either side of us herds of antelope continually sported, and in the valley black-tailed deer were not uncommon. In the precipitous and rugged mountains that we encountered we found the big-horn more numerous than in any other locality that we passed.

Following down Williams' river, with these interesting animals still for our companions, we continued our march towards the great river of the west. The beautiful stream sometimes emerged suddenly from the earth a bold rivulet, leaping playfully over its gravelly bed for several miles, and then would as suddenly disappear again beneath the sand. Whether creeping slowly among the bushes or passing through the open valley, we ever found something to please and interest us. The birds, however, of this region were particularly interesting. Myriads of ducks and geese were continually frightened from the stream or neighboring lagoons, of which a large number of interesting specimens were added to our collection. Among the smaller birds, which were also very numerous, we found several new and exceedingly interesting ones. At no other locality did we meet with such great success in collecting new and undescribed species, not only of birds, but also of reptiles and fishes. In this stream we found great numbers of the latter, comprising a variety of species not before observed.

From the Great Colorado river to the Pacific.—Travelling up the Colorado for some distance, we found its shores peopled by hundreds of Indians, whose friendly manifestations made us soon feel quite at home among them. Besides assisting us in many other ways, they also enabled us to procure some species both of fishes and birds, which, without their aid, we probably could not have captured. Thus our stay among them was made both pleasant and profitable. The birds and fishes constitute the most important features of natural history immediately in the vicinity of our route. The larger animals, being closely hunted, were scarce.

Crossing the river and accompanied by several Mojave Indians as guides, we continued our march towards the Pacific. From this point we saw but little of interest before reaching the Mojave river. Grass being scarce, except in the vicinity of the few watering places, we had but few companions during our long and tiresome marches, save the raven, which hovered over our now fast failing mules, and added to our dreary feelings by his hoarse croaks. Occasionally, too, the jackass rabbit would spring from his hiding place among the stinking larrea and hurry off. Frequently we found this animal far away from any water known to our guides. Sometimes, also, while encamped in this less-favored region, the cayote, attracted by our camp fires, would approach and serenade us as he had done before.

Near the watering places on our route, we frequently saw signs of the big-horn and other animals, where, watched by the Indians when coming to slake their thirst, they had been killed. It was not until after we had reached the Mojave river, however, that we met with much success in collecting specimens. Here, in addition to the many small birds that were continually singing around us, and the numerous ducks that were scared from the marshes, we found the stream itself inhabited by several species of fishes. Many of these we added to our collection; as also of the reptiles which here abounded. Approaching the mountain, we once more found the black-tailed deer and grizzly bear; one feeding in the green valleys, the other among the pines on the rugged slopes.

From this point our route lay along the beautiful valley of the San Gabriel river. Here we found the green pastures dotted by flocks of sheep and herds of cattle. Game of the larger kind was, of course, scarce through this region, being closely hunted by the inhabitants; but we found birds here of almost every variety of plumage, and many quadrupeds of the smaller species. Many of these we added to our collection before reaching Los Angeles, where we ceased our labors for a while, and enjoyed those comforts of which we had been so long deprived.

We were agreeably disappointed in regard to the abundance and character of the game of the country traversed. It will be seen from the foregoing statement that we were almost continually within reach of deer, antelope, and hare. Still, it would not be safe to depend upon game for subsistence in passing over the line, especially in the case of a large party. As is well known, all the animals just mentioned are easily driven off from their usual range by frequent interruptions, and at all times a skilful hunter is required to capture them. The case is different with the buffalo, whose presence in a certain region is more to be calculated upon, and when seen is more readily captured, affording at the same time a much larger amount of food to each head.

Before concluding, I have the honor to present to your notice a summary statement of the number and variety of the specimens of natural history collected by Mr. H. B. Möllhausen and myself, between the Rio Grande and the Pacific ocean. Besides the collection herein mentioned, two other very extensive ones were made: one by Mr. Möllhausen, between Fort Smith, Arkansas, and Albuquerque, New Mexico; the other by myself, between Indianola, Texas, and Albuquerque, New Mexico. These were sent from the latter place to Washington, where they arrived safely, after a delay of several months on the prairies between Santa Fé and Independence, and are now deposited in the Smithsonian Institution, (together with the one which is the subject of this report,) to the credit of the expedition, having been also assorted and properly labelled.

In the following statement, the numbers used correspond to those attached to the specimens, and where a note or remark is wanting, it may be an indication, generally, that one may be found in another place, where the species are discussed separately.

STATEMENT.

No. of Label.	Locality.
No. 1. Anser hutchinsi	Rio Rito, N. M.
2. Querquedula carolinensis	do. do.
3. Querquedula carolinensis	do. do.
4. Skull of an Indian	Laguna, N. M.
5. Fishes	Rio Gallo, N. M.
6. Lepus artemesiæ	Sierra Madre, N. M.
(*a*) Spermophilus harrisii	Sierra Madre, N. M.

This beautiful and rare spermophile is found in considerable numbers at Cold Spring, near the summit of the Sierra Madre. In this vicinity there were vast piles of scoriacious volcanic rock, in which it lived. It was not very shy, but a specimen was procured with difficulty, from the fact that it was almost impossible to kill the animal so dead, without spoiling completely the skin, that it could not crawl into the rocks beyond our reach before overtaken. Its food in this locality consisted of acorns and *piñones,* the fruit of the *Pinus edulis.* We again observed this animal near camp 139, between the Great Colorado and Mojave rivers. Here we found it on the hill-sides in the most rocky and inaccessible spots, and exceedingly shy. A specimen was procured only by secreting myself in the vicinity of the hole into which it escaped, and patiently watching an hour or more for its appearance.

No. 7. Fishes	Rio Piscado, N. M.
8. Rana*	do. do.

In many places in this creek there was much grass and moss and large masses of confervae floating on its surface. In such spots we found very many frogs, apparently all of the same species, but believed to be undescribed. The weather was unusually cold for the season (November), and these animals being completely chilled and torpid, were easily caught. The Zuñi Indians look upon them as sacred objects, believing them to be the preservers of the springs and possessing the power of keeping the supply of water in dry seasons. Their vessels are ornamented with rude paintings of this animal, and they are said to hold a grand feast once a year in honor of it. So strenuously did they remonstrate when they observed us taking them that we desisted until an opportunity offered when there were no Indians present.

* This specimen and others that follow, not having their species named, were lost upon the passage across the isthmus, and hence their characteristics were undetermined.

Nos. 9, 10, 11, 12, 13. Fishes.................Zuñi river, N. M.

The Zuñi river is a small stream of pure, clear water, emptying into the Little Colorado. We took fishes from it at several different localities, and found among them at least four distinct species; two of which we recognized as the *Gila robusta* and *Gila gracilis*, the latter being by far the most numerous. The others were believed to be new to science.

No. 14. Spiza ciris.....................................75 miles west of Albuquerque, N. M.
15. Milvulus forficatus........................... do. do. do.
(a) Sialia occidentalis........................... do. do. do.
(b) Carpodacus cassinii (n. s.*)............... do. do. do.
16. Xanthornus affinis.......................... do. do. do.
(a) Carpodacus pileatus.......................... do. do. do.
17. Picicorous Columbianus......................95 do. do. do.
(a) Spiza ciris..................................... do. do. do.
18. Gymnokitta cyanocephala .... do. do. do.
19. Ptiliogonys townsendii..................... do. do. do.
20. Cyanocitta macrolopha (n. s.)............100 do. do. do.
21. Agelaius phoeniceus........................ do. do. do.
22. Cyanocitta macrolopha (n. s.)........... do. do. do.
23. Agelaius phoeniceus......................... do. do. do.
24. Sitta carolinensis............................ do. do. do.
25. Archibuteo lagopus.......................... do. do. do.
26. Otocoris chrysolaemus......................Near Zuñi, N. M.
27. Do. do. .... do. do.
28. Fish..Little Colorado river, N. M.

Although we were encamped on this stream at several places for some days, and although we searched it thoroughly, we were obliged to content ourselves with a single specimen. The absence of fishes at these places may, probably, be accounted for to some extent by the character of the stream itself. Its waters were loaded with sand, which was carried rapidly along by the current; besides, it was generally shallow, and offered no quiet pools as resting places; nor was there any grass or weeds or bushes in it, but its bottom was a continuous quicksand. The specimen procured measured about three inches in length; general color, white and silvery, with very small scales, belonging to the sucker family, but its genus was unknown.

No. 29. Ptiliogonys townsendii...................Near Zuñi, N. M.
30. Struthus Oregonus.......................... do. do.
31. Mimus montanus............................. do. do.
32. Geococcyx viaticus..........................First camp on L. Colorado river, N. M.
33. Geococcyx viaticus..........................Third camp do. do.
34. Pica hudsonica ....Fourth camp do. do.
35. Picus harrassii................................ do. do. do.
36. Psaltria plumbea (n. s.)...................Sixth camp do. do.
37. Querquedula Carolinensis................. do. do. do.
38. Falco polyagrus.............................. do. do. do.
39. Spizella Canadensis .... do. do. do.
40. Psaltria plumbea (n. s.) .... do. do. do.
41. Psaltria plumbea (n. s.) .... do. do. do.
42. Spizella Canadensis .... do. do. do.
43. Sitta pygmaea................................San Francisco Mts., N. M.

* (N. S.) This indicates that the species is new to science.

44. Zonotrichia fallax............................Camp 97.
45. Callipepla gambeli........... ....Camp 97.
46. Bubo magellanicus.. ....Camp 98.
47. Certhia Americana..........................Pueblo creek N. M.
48. Carpodacus pileatus.......................... do. do.
(a.) Sturnella neglecta.......................... do. do.
(b.) Sturnella neglecta.......................... do. do.
49. Pipilo Oregonus............................. do. do.
50. Lophophanes wollweberi .... do. do.
(a.) Aguelaius gubernator. .... do. do.
51. Aguelaius gubernator .... do. do.
52. Sialia occidentalis............................ do. do.
(a.) Carpodacus Cassinii (n. s.) .... do. do.
53. Cyanocitta macrolopha (n. s.) ....Camp 105.
(a.) Strigiceps uliginosus .... do.
54. Tinnunculus sparverius .... do.
55. Regulus calendula............................ do.
56. Regulus calendula........................... do.
57. Otus Americanus............................Camp 107.
58. Corvus splendens (?) ....Camp 110.
59. Sialia occidentalis .. .. do.
60. Sialia occidentalis .... do.
61. Zonotrichia leucophrys.....................Camp 111.
62. Zonotrichia leucophrys..................... do.
63. Psaltria plumbea (n. s.) .... do.
64. Zonotrichia leucophrys..................... do.
65. Zonotrichia leucophrys..................... do.
66. Thryothorus Mexicanus....................Camp 112.
67. Culicivora plumbea (n. s.) ....Williams' river, N. M.
68. Thryothorus obsoletus...................... do. do.
69. Ptiliogonys nitens........................... do. do.
70. Pipilo mesoleucus (n. s.) .... do. do.
71. Buteo swainsoni..............................Camp 114, Williams' river, N. M.
72. Pipilo aberti .... do. do. do.
73. Corvus splendens (?) ....Camp 115, do. do.
74. Chrysomitris psaltria.......................Camp 116, do. do.
75. Regulus calendula........................... do. do. do.
76. Chrysomitris psaltria .... do. do. do.
77. Querquedula Carolinensis................. do. do. do.
78. Chrysomitris psaltria....................... do. do. do.
79. Selasphorus costae ....Camp 117, do. do.
80. Selasphorus costae .... do. do. do.
81. Charadrius vociferus........................ do. do. do.
82. Sturnella neglecta........................... do. do. do.
83. Mimus polyglottus .... do. do. do.
84. Scops —— ....Camp 118, do. do.
85. Querquedula Carolinensis.................. do. do. do.
86. Carpodacus familiaris....................... do. do. do.
87. Carpodacus familiaris....................... do. do. do.
88. Tyrannula sayi................................ do. do. do.
89. Clangula albeola ....Camp 119, do. do.

No. 90. Mimus montanus..........................Camp 119, Williams' river, N. M.
91. Culicivora plumbea?,....................... do. do. do.
92. Pipilo aberti..................................Camp 120, do. do.
93. Mimus montanus.......................... do. do. do.
94. Psaltria plumbea............................ do. do. do.
95. Pipilo mesoleucus.......................... do. do. do.
96. Ptiliogonys nitens.......................... do. do. do.
97. Chrysomitris psaltria...................... do. do. do.
(*a.*) Bubo magellanicus......................... do. do. do.
98. Charadrius vociferus....................... do. do. do.
99. Centurus uropygialis (n. s.)............. do. do. do.
100. Peucæa lincolnlii........................... do. do. do.
101. Pipilo aberti................................. do. do. do.
102. Lepus callotis?..............................Camp 97, Little Colorado river, N. M.

This species was found in greater numbers at the above-mentioned locality than elsewhere on the route. The valley at this point was covered by tall and coarse grass which grew in bunches, varying in size from a foot in diameter at the base, to several feet or even yards; there being always between them a narrow and tortuous, but clean pathway. In this grass this hare was generally found; rarely going to the hills; and the roots and tender shoots seemed to afford it food.

No. 103. Hystrix Canadensis.........................Little Colorado river, N. M.
105. Neotoma ——...............................Little Colorado river, N. M.

These animals were numerous in many places in the valley of this river. They lived in the sand in very tortuous holes, and extending for many yrds, though rarely more than fifteen inches below the surface. The entrance to their abode was generally in a pile of earth heaped around the base of a mezquite bush, (*Algarobia,*) upon the roots of which it seemed to feed. So far as we noticed, they were entirely nocturnal in their habits. On several occasions we attempted to dig them out with spades, but were always forced, after hours of labor, to relinquish the task without having accomplished our purpose. The specimen procured had, during the night, gotten into an empty bucket, from which it could not get out, and was captured alive in the morning. The body measured about three and a half inches, and the tail the same; the hair was coarser and darker than that of some others of the same genus noticed.

No. 106 Arvicola......................................Camp 94.
(*a*) Arvicola.......................................Camp 94.
(*b* Arvicola..Camp 94.

These three specimens were caught at New Year Spring. Here was a luxuriant growth of gramma grass, (*Boutelerea,*) both in the valley and on the hill-sides. On the latter places were many loose fragments of volcanic rocks of various sizes scattered about, but not in such quantities as to materially interfere with the growth of the grass. In this locality the specimens were found. They built their nests under the stones, and constructed them of dry grass in a manner similar to those of the common meadow mouse, (*Arvicola riparius,*) and, like this animal, had also paths under the grass, diverging in every direction from its hole; and, indeed, its general appearance was very much like that animal, and seemed only to differ from it in size, the specimens being decidedly smaller.

No. 107. Neotoma?....................................Camp 96.

This animal was found in a country covered by a growth of the rough-barked cedar, (*Juniperus pachydermata.*) They seem to select a hollow tree with a hole near the root; then around it they pile vast heaps of dry twigs, and fragments of the several species of cactaceæ (*Opuntia*) which grow here. The latter is probably a protection against the depredations of wolves. Numerous lodges of this kind were found throughout the forest, into one of which we dug until we reached the hole at the root of the tree; when, applying a match, we soon compelled the animal to leave it, which it did by finding its way out several feet above, and fell to the ground apparently dead. The food of this animal seems to consist mainly of the fruit of the cactus.

No. (*a*) ——— ———. (Mouse)....................Camp 96.

This animal closely resembled the common field-mouse, (*Hesperomys*,) though somewhat larger; the ears, also, being somewhat larger in proportion to the size of the animal. Its abdomen was white, the same color extending slightly on each side; the feet perfectly white; the tail very long and hairy. It lived in the hollows of the cedar trees, like the subject of the preceding description, (107,) and also built up around the root of the tree a pile of small dry twigs. Sometimes as many as three were found living together in the same tree.

No. 108. Lepus artemesiæ..........................Camp 99, Picacho mountains, New Mexico.
109. Hystrix Canadensis........................Little Colorado river, New Mexico.
110. Neotoma....................................Camp 106.
111. Dipodomys ordii..........................Camp 106.

In removing the cloth which was used in our tent as a carpet, this animal was found under it. No hole was observed in the ground within the tent, from which it could have come, nor did it attempt to make its escape into one; but when pursued, leaped wildly and rapidly about, making at each bound an astonishing distance. Its hind legs, being very long and muscular, are well adapted for this mode of locomotion.

No. 112. ——— ———. (Lizard)................Camp 110, New Mexico.
(*a*) ——— ———. (Lizard)................Camp 110, New Mexico.
113. ——— ———. (Lizard)................Camp 111, New Mexico.
(*a*) ——— ———. (Lizard)................Camp 111, New Mexico.
114. ——— ———. (Lizard)................Camp 111, New Mexico.
(*a*) Rana ———..............................Camp 111, New Mexico.
115. ——— ———. (Lizard)................White Cliff creek, New Mexico.
(*a*) ——— ———. (Lizard)................White Cliff creek, New Mexico.
(*b*) Neotoma ——. White Cliff creek, New Mexico.

This was much the largest species of this genus that we saw. We found around a pile of rotten drift-wood near the creek, tracks and other evidences of the presence of some mammalia, and applying a match to the bushes, we patiently awaited the result; and when nearly the entire pile was consumed, the specimen came out, having four young ones adhering to it. The little ones were very young; and after the mother was killed, they were placed in an open spot on the sand, where they crawled awkwardly about for a while, uttering all the time a plaintive, whining cry, not unlike that of a very young kitten. They were caught early in February.

No. 116. Rana...Camp 113, Williams' river, New Mexico.
117, 118, 134, 136, 141, 143, 144, 147. } Fishes.................Williams' river, New Mexico.

The several lots of fishes enumerated above were taken at various times, at different localities, during our march down Bill Williams' fork. This stream frequently entirely disappears in the sand; but where it flows, is generally a bold and rapid rivulet of clear, pure water. The fishes which we took from it comprised at least five distinct species, and probably six or seven, among which were recognized the *Gila robusta* and *Gila elegans;* and of these two, the former species was the most abundant. The others were probably entirely new and undescribed.

No. 118 (*a.*) ——— ——— ....(Lizard)............ Williams' river.
(*b.*) Scolopendra ——— .... Williams' river.
119. Spermophilus ——— ....Camp 117, Williams' river.

This animal was found among the rocks on the hill sides in the immediate vicinity of the creek. It was very active, and ran with great rapidity. It was somewhat larger than the *Spermophilus tridecem-lineatus;* its color a uniform rusty gray, its belly being of a lighter color. Its hair was rather coarse; its tail short and bushy. Two specimens were observed in this locality, one of which only was procured; but at no other locality on the route was another observed.

No. 119 (*a.*) Geomys ——— ....Camp 117, Williams' river, N. M.
120. ——— ——— (Lizard) ....Camp 119 do. do.
(*a.*) ——— ——— (Lizard) .... do. do. do.
121. ——— ——— (Lizard) ....Camp 121 do. do.
(*a.*) ——— ——— (Snake).................. do. do. do.
122. Lepus callotis (?) .... do. do. do.
123. Bufo ——— ....Camp 125 do. do.
(*a.*) Bufo ——— .... do. do. do.

These toads were quite common at many points along this creek, and were generally found among the bushes or on sandy spots, though sometimes observed in the water. They were all small, the usual length of the body being about two inches, including the outstretched hindlegs about 3½ inches.

(*b.*) Perognathus ——— ....Camp 125, Williams' river, N. M.

This was an extremely rare animal. The specimen procured was probably *Perognathus flavus*, at least in size and general appearance it very closely resembled it.

124. Phrynosoma ——— ....Camp 128, Great Colorado river.
(*a.*) Do. ——— .... do. do. do.
(*b.*) Do. ——— .... do. do. do.
(*c.*) Do. ——— .... do. do. do.
(*d.*) Gila elegans................................ do. do. do.
(*e.*) ——— ——— (Lizard.)................ do. do. do.
125. ——— ——— (Rat.)...................... do. do. do.
(*a.*) Crotaphytus ——— .... do. do. do.

This large lizard was found on the side of the mountain, and when observed was stretched out on a rock, apparently enjoying the heat of the sun. While in this position it was approached by an Indian and shot with an arrow. Although it was the only specimen seen, we learned from the Pah-Utahs that it was not an uncommon animal in this locality, and was prized by them as an article of food.

No. 126. ——— ——— (Lizard.)................Camp 131.
(*a.*) ——— ——— (Lizard.)................ do.
(*b.*) Phrynosoma ——— .... do.
(*c.*) Do. ——— .... do.
127. ——— ——— (Rat.)...................... do.
128. ——— ——— (Lizard.)................Camp 133.
(*a.*) ——— ——— (Lizard.)................ do.
(*b.*) ——— ——— (Lizard.)................ do.
129. Phrynosoma ——— ....Camp 144.
(*a.*) Do. ——— .... do.
(*b.*) Crotalus ——— .... do.
130. Phrynosoma ——— ....Camp 147, Mojave river, Cal
(*a.*) Do. ——— .... do. do.

(b.) Hesperomys ——— ....Camp 147, Mojave river, Cal.
131. ——— ——— (Snake.)..................Camp 149, do.
132. Fishes.................................Camp 146, do.

This stream rises in the coast range of mountains, and flows towards the Great Colorado, but probably sinks in the sand long before reaching that river, Where we saw it, it was a bold rivulet of clear and pure water. The lot of fishes taken from it comprised about three species, probably all new to science.

No 133. Fishes ....Great Colorado river.

We did not observe more than two species of fishes in this stream, one of which was the *Gila elegans*, the other unknown.

No. 135. Fishes......................................Pueblo creek, New Mexico.

This was the most beautiful mountain stream that we observed on our journey. Its pure and clear water came tumbling and bubbling over the rocks in such a manner as to forcibly remind us of the mountain brooks of the Atlantic States. It probably empties into the San Francisco river. From it we obtained a single species of fish, the largest specimen not being more than 2 or $2\frac{1}{2}$ inches in length.

No. 137. ——— ———. (Lizard)................Cajon Pass, California.
138. Hesperomys ———. ....Williams' river, New Mexico.
(a.) Hesperomys ———. ....Williams' river, New Mexico.
139. ——— ———. (Snake)....................Great Colorado river.
(a.) Hesperomys ———. ....Great Colorado river.
140. Neotoma ———. ....San Francisco mountains, New Mexico.
142. Rana ———. ....Camp 134, Williams' river, New Mexico.
(a.) ——— ———. (Shells).....................Camp 134, Williams' river, New Mexico.
145. Neotoma ———. ....San Francisco mountains, New Mexico.
146. Neotoma ———. ....Camp 90.
148. Scorpio ———. ....Williams' river.
151. Crotalophorus ———. ....Little Colorado river.
152. Rana ———. ....White Cliff creek, New Mexico.
(a.) Rana ———. ....White Cliff creek, New Mexico.

This tributary of Williams' river is a stream of clear and pure water, and the frogs here obtained are probably identical with those obtained from that stream.

No. 153. Hesperomys ———. ....Head waters of Williams' river.
(a.) Hesperomys ———. ....Head waters of Williams' river.
154. Neotoma ———. ....Great Colorado river.
155. Geomys fulvus..............................Camp 99, Picacho mountains, New Mexico.
156. Sciurus aberti...............................San Francisco mountains, New Mexico.
(a.) Sciurus aberti ....San Francisco mountains, New Mexico.
(b.) Sciurus aberti ....San Francisco mountains, New Mexico.

This beautiful squirrel was very common in the San Francisco range of mountains, living among the tall pines that here abound, and finding its chief subsistence in the *piñones*, the fruit of the *Pinus edulis*. We did not observe it farther west than Mount Sitgreaves.

No. 157. Spermophilus beecheyii...................Cocomongo Rancho, California.
(a.) Spermophilus beecheyii.......................Cocomongo Rancho, California.
(b.) Spermophilus beecheyii.......................Cocomongo Rancho, California.

These singular animals are very numerous near the Cocomongo Rancho, and, indeed, throughout the valley of the San Gabriel river. They were always found living in communities, and in their habits, generally, very closely resembled the prairie dog, (*Cynomys ludovicianus.*) Their size is about that of the common grey squirrel, (*Sciurus carolinensis*,) or perhaps a little larger. Their color is usually a rustyish gray, and varying from that to very dark; I have seen some specimens almost black. The owl, (*Athene hypogœa,*) which is the constant companion of the prairie dog, was also found among these animals in considerable numbers.

No. 158. Mephitis ———. ....Camp 104, Pueblo creek, New Mexico.

This skunk was intermediate in size between the common *Mephitis chinga* and the *Mephitis zorilla* of Mexico. Its general color was black, with a white line on each side, white forehead, and the tip of the tail white. It was the only specimen observed.

No. 159. Skull of a Navajo Indian................Fort Defiance, New Mexico.
160. Human skull................................Found on Williams' river, New Mexico.
161. Ovis montana, (skull of female)....... do. do. do.
162. Canis latrans, (skin) .... do. do. do.
163. Antilocapra Americana, (skin).........San Francisco mountains, New Mexico.
164. Ovis aries, (skull)..........................New Mexico.

This specimen was procured on account of its peculiarity in having four horns, that are well developed, being about eight inches in length; one on each side erect, and one turned downwards. It is said that, many years ago, the proprietor of an extensive hacienda on the Rio Grande owned a vast number of sheep possessing this peculiarity, and that the number of horns to each individual was never less than three, and often as many as seven. His flock was driven off by the Navajo Indians, who still graze large numbers of these animals in the mountains of New Mexico, and among which exist many anomalies of this kind.

No. 165. Picus scalaris ....Camp 122.
166. Pterocyanea cæruleata ....Camp 123.
167. Scolopax Wilsonii........................... do.
168. Scolopax Wilsonii........................... do.
169. Cypselus melanoleucus, (n. s.)........... do.
170. Tyrannula sayi............................... do.
171. Centurus uropygialis, (n. s.)............. do.
172. Dafila acuta ....Camp 126.
173. Sturnella neglecta........................... do.
174. Spizella pallida ....Camp 127.
175. Coturniculus passerinus.................... do.
176. Cotyle serripennis....... ....Camp 128.
177. Antrostomus nuttalli.......................Camp 130.
178. Lanius ludovicianus......................... do.
179. Morphnus unicinctus ....Camp 134.
180. Colaptes rubricatus?........................ do.
182. Pterocyanea cæruleata ....Mojave river, California.
183. Callipepla Californica .... do. do.
184. Totanus melanoleucus...................... do. do.
185. Buteo montanus.............................. do. do.
186. Cyanocitta Californica..................... do. do.
187. Agelaius gubernator........................Cocomongo Rancho, California.
188. Agelaius gubernator........................ do. do.
189. Tyrannula nigricans......................... do. do.
190. Sylvicola Auduboni.......................... do. do.
191. Athene hypogæa.............................Los Angeles, California.
192. Aix sponsa.....................................San Francisco, California.
193. Chaulelasmus streperus.................... do. do.
194. Fuligula mariloides..... .... do. do.

195. Numenius longirostris......................San Francisco, California.
196. Rallus elegans................................ do. do.
(a.) Ibis ordii....................................... do. do.
197. Ovis montana.......(skull of male)......San Francisco mountains, New Mexico.
198. Canis latrans........(skull)................Williams' river, New Mexico.

A single glance at the foregoing statement is sufficient to convince us that the collection was a very extensive one, and possessed of rare interest. The country traversed by the expedition was almost entirely unexplored, and afforded an opportunity for scientific research but seldom offered; and we strenuously endeavored to make as complete a zoological collection as we could, by procuring and preserving everything within our reach; and after reaching Los Angeles, in looking over the specimens, and finding among them so many things new to science, felt ourselves fully and richly rewarded for any trouble or labor that we may have undergone in obtaining them. At that place nearly the entire alcoholic collection, for convenience of transportation, was repacked and placed in a large keg. And it becomes my painful duty to report, that this keg, containing, as it did, many of our most valuable specimens, was lost at Panama, through the negligence of Hinckley's Express Company, to the agent of which it was turned over for transportation to Aspinwall; and, notwithstanding our efforts to recover it have been unceasing up to the present time, we have been entirely unsuccessful; nor have we even been able to elicit any information concerning it. It contained the specimens corresponding to the following numbers, viz: 5, 6, (*a*,) 7, 8, 9, 10, 11, 12, 13, 28, 102, 105, 106, (*a*,) (*b*,) 107, (*a*,) 108, 110, 111, 112, (*a*,) 113, (*a*,) 114, (*a*,) 115, (*a*,) (*b*,) 124, (*a*,) (*b*,) (*c*,) (*d*,) (*e*,) 125, (*a*,) 126, (*a*,) (*b*,) (*c*,) 127, 128, (*a*,) (*b*,) (*c*,) 129, (*a*,) (*b*,) 130, (*a*,) (*b*,) 131, 132, 133, 134, 135, 136, 137, 138, (*a*,) 139, (*a*,) 140, 141, 142, (*a*,) (*b*,) 143, 144, 145, 146, 147, 148, 149, 151, 152, (*a*,) 153, (*a*,) 154, 155, 156, (*a*,) (*b*,) 157, (*a*,) (*b*,) 158. It will be perceived from the foregoing that, through this negligence, not only the expedition has suffered very seriously, but that science itself has met with an almost irreparable loss; which, we are sure, no one will regret more earnestly than yourself, knowing, as we do, the lively interest that you have always manifested in this department, and your untiring efforts to promote its success.

In conclusion, allow me to state that, in making collections in natural history, I was very kindly and continually assisted by Mr. Möllhausen, to whose zeal and industry equal credit with myself is due for the number and variety of specimens.

Very respectfully, your obedient servant,

C. B. R. KENNERLY, M. D.,
Physician and Naturalist to the Expedition.

A. W. WHIPPLE,
First Lieut. Topographical Engineers, U. S. A.,
In charge of exploration for railroad route near 35th parallel.

NOTE.

The remainder of the Zoological Report will appear in a subsequent volume, it being impossible to prepare it in time for publication in connexion with the other portions of this report.

www.ingramcontent.com/pod-product-compliance
Lightning Source LLC
LaVergne TN
LVHW020636110826
845149LV00004B/1221

* 9 7 8 1 4 1 8 1 9 1 0 9 2 *